D1244432

THE BEATLES

the summer of 1968

'BEATLES BY THE RIVER'

The photograph on the front cover of this book is available as a limited edition print entitled 'Beatles by the River'.
Limited to an issue of 500, each photograph will be printed to order under supervision of the photographer, Tom Murray.
Tom will sign and number each print on the border. The edition will appear in 8" x11" format with a full colour glossy finish. Each print will be accompanied by a signed certificate of authenticity.

£50.00 plus p & p

the summer of 1968

1968 was the most significant year in the Beatles' career. Between the first TV screening of the *Magical Mystery Tour* home-movie at Christmas 1967, and the beginning of the *Get Back/Let It Be* sessions in January 1969, they made all the decisions that would seal not only the fate of the group, but also the future direction of their four individual careers over the next decade.

As a quartet, 1968 was the year when the Beatles recorded their sprawling, brilliant, self-indulgent and ultimately magnificent double 'White Album'. They launched an equally sprawling and self-indulgent multi-media corporation, Apple. They appointed themselves talent-spotters and creative nurses for a generation. They allowed their business affairs to tumble into chaos. They gradually forced apart the tight-knit comradeship which had always been their greatest strength.

John Lennon and Yoko Ono became tempestuous partners for life. Linda Eastman drew Paul McCartney away from his promiscuous bachelor lifestyle. Ringo Starr became the first Beatle to leave the group, but was persuaded to rejoin. He also inaugurated his solo career as a film actor. George Harrison completed his first full-length work in the field of Indian music.

And there was more:

John Lennon fell victim to drug abuse. He also left his colleagues in no doubt that they were no longer the most important factor in his life. Neither was his wife, Cynthia; the couple were divorced in 1968. Likewise, Paul McCartney's engagement to actress Jane Asher collapsed. And least predictable of all, the Beatles devoted several weeks to exploring the spiritual potential of Transcendental Meditation, not in their own backyards but in the Himalayan retreat of Rishikesh. Then, while Western Europe and the U.S. were rocked by student riots, the Beatles returned home to reveal that their guru, the ever-beaming Maharishi Mahesh Yogi, had turned out to be a sorry disappointment, but that the answer to all life's problems was still within you rather than without you.

It was a year that began with the rare, almost unbelievable experience of failure, and ended with the false hope of a new dawn. After the worldwide critical acclaim for the *Sgt. Pepper* album in 1967, the Beatles must have believed that they were infallible. But the unexpected death of their increasingly tortured manager, Brian Epstein, that August, robbed them of vital stability. His role had become little more than token by the time of his death, but his very existence ensured that the Beatles would never pursue any idle whim into excess. Without him, the group were subject to any idea, no matter how batty, which any one of the members could impose on the others.

Epstein might not have prevented *Magical Mystery Tour*, their flamboyant, stoned and defiantly non-commercial movie, from being made, but if he had still been alive, you can be certain that it wouldn't have been lampooned across the media. He'd have pulled some strings, leaned on the Beatles to make sure that they abandoned their scheme of creating avant-garde TV for prime-time viewing, and generally prepared the way for a piece of celluloid that was actually highly promising but wasn't exactly ideal mainstream fare for sleepy Boxing Day evening.

Without Epstein to create the proper climate, *Magical Mystery Tour* flopped into the holiday TV schedules like a deflated soufflé. The press fall-out astonished and hurt the Beatles, especially Paul McCartney, who thereafter drew sharply back from creating anything too experimental. He'd been the 'avant-garde Beatle' for two years or more, leading Lennon and the others into dabbling with collages of sound and vision, and hanging out in London's West End with the pick of the capital's young poets, film-makers and writers. *Magical Mystery Tour* put paid to that.

The Beatles had assumed that their first self-made movie would be so successful that they'd automatically slide into more of the same. When it flopped, all their plans for a tie-in film with *Sgt. Pepper* were finally abandoned. In its wake was nothing more concrete than a general agreement to make another album later in the year, and an equally vague plan to extend their initial contact with Transcendental Meditation into a prolonged period of personal tuition with the master Maharishi himself.

From the start, insiders and outsiders watched the guru's increasing influence over the Beatles with some scepticism. The group were nothing if not enthusiasts, and they responded to the emotional and spiritual pull of Transcendental Meditation with the evangelical fervour which they had previously used to advertise the merits of Chuck Berry's rock'n'roll, Bob Dylan's songwriting, and the creative benefits of LSD.

Once again, Epstein's guiding hand was sorely missed. He'd been effectively out of action when the group had first discovered the Maharishi, sunk in depression in his London flat. Then his death had interrupted their initial weekend of TM study. Now there was no one strong enough to persuade the group that their spiritual adviser might not only have their personal growth in mind.

The Beatles were certainly whole-hearted in their enthusiasm for the guru, as Peter Brown - a long-time employee of Epstein's NEMS organisation, who was carried forward with The Beatles into the hierarchy of Apple - witnessed at first hand. He reported in his biography of the group that there was talk of the Fab Four financing a movie about the Maharishi. And that wasn't all: 'One day I received a call from the lawyers for ABC Television in America. They said that the Maharishi had been negotiating with them for a TV special that he said would include an appearance by the Beatles." When Brown passed this information on to his bosses, they denied all knowledge of the TV special, but refused to let any cynicism taint their enthusiasm for the guru.

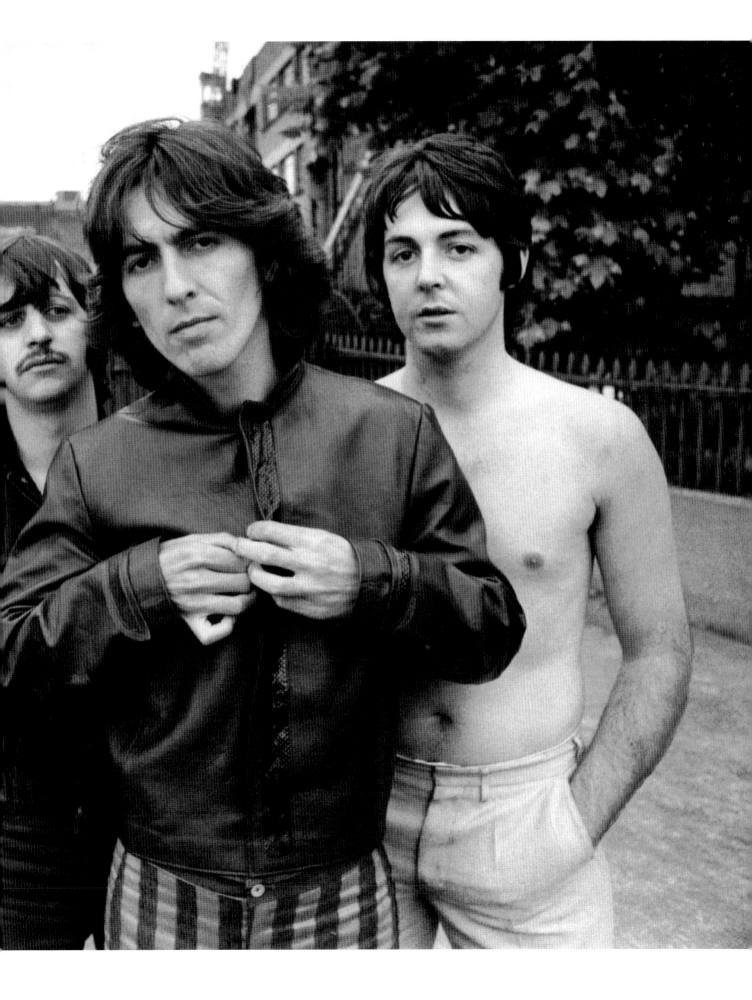

Before their departure, there was the small matter of a single to be recorded.

McCartney's 'Lady Madonna' returned the group to their rock'n'roll and R&B roots, while Harrison's spiritual influence on the rest of the Beatles over the previous two years was acknowledged when Lennon and McCartney finally allowed one of his songs, 'The Inner Light', onto the B-side. Meanwhile, one of Lennon's finest compositions, 'Across The Universe', was immediately earmarked for a World Wildlife Fund charity album, removing it for consideration on any subsequent 1968 Beatles releases.

When the time came to make a promotional film for 'Lady Madonna', the Beatles used the time constructively, assembling Lennon's 'Hey Bulldog' in rapid time. As Lennon expert and critic John Robertson subsequently noted, the song's lyrics "trod a fine line between nonsense and inspired nonsense, and the gusto of the performance, and the sheer chaos of the fade-out, made this one of the warmest, most enjoyable Beatles recordings of the era." But Robertson also saw the freewheeling anarchy of the session in more portentous terms: "In a way, it was another milestone on the road to dissolution. Rarely in the future would they approach a session with such boyish enthusiasm. The disillusionment of the Rishikesh fiasco seemed to remove the last of the group's Four Musketeers spirit, that one-for-all camaraderie and mutual support which had seen them through every crisis from the sacking of Pete Best to the critical panning of *Magical Mystery Tour*."

The Beatles were certainly searching for a direction,

and a spiritual guide for the journey, in the early months of 1968. Uniquely placed to watch their uncertain progress in the months after Epstein's death, but before the advent of 'John & Yoko', was the official Beatles biographer, Hunter Davies. His view of life with the Lennons at this point was certainly telling: "John spends most of his time, when he's not recording or writing a song, curled up on a small sofa, doing nothing. The sofa is far too small for him. He would obviously be more comfortable on one of the lush ones from the other room. But he curls his legs round, and can lie for hours. When it's fine, he opens the sliding glass door and goes out and sits on a step in the garden, looking down at his swimming pool and his English country garden."

Davies also acutely noticed the shift in the group's internal politics, which had seen Lennon, the unquestioned leader through the Beatlemania era, gradually sidelined through a mixture of McCartney's ambitiousness and his own ennui. Davies described Paul as "the businessman, the pusher", the one whose energy and enthusiasm was vital to persuade the rest of the Beatles to see their projects through.

The whole Apple idea and impetus is Paul's," Davies realised, though he pointed out that the remainder of the group were always on hand to discuss major decisions. He described Paul's concept of the multi-media company as " a big corporation, with shops, clubs, studios and the best people in the business, from cameramen and engineers to artists, writers and composers.

But as with the Maharishi episode, it was the youngest Beatle, George Harrison, who assumed control of the group for the first — and as it transpired, last — time. Davies noted perceptively that "George today is the Beatle who needs the other Beatles least", who was happiest to pursue his own creative and spiritual interests outside the security of the group. Despite his reputation in early years as "the businessman Beatle", the one who would question Brian Epstein closest about the small financial print in their contracts, George's new interests were far removed from the material world. Hunter Davies reported that "George spends at least three hours a day practising his sitar" - something that might be vaguely useful for the Beatles, but was hardly guaranteed in itself to generate a fortune.

It was Harrison's total immersion in the Indian spiritual experience, either via meditation, prayer or the study of the sitar, that set the tone for the Beatles' visit to India. Over the course of two months in the spring of 1968, their quest for enlightenment, and their cynical disillusionment when nirvana collapsed into near-chaos, triggered the major events which littered the rest of the year — the collapse of Lennon's marriage and McCartney's engagement, and the dissolution of the collective spirit which had maintained the Beatles through every crisis to date. The fact that the trauma resulted in what was probably their finest album did not necessarily offer them much consolation.

The group's journey to the Maharishi's village in Rishikesh, high in the Himalayas, mirrored their slow shedding of Western values. They flew to India on a jet, then transferred to a taxi and an ageing jeep. A team of donkeys, no less, led them to within a mile of the camp; but the final trek, across a narrow, precarious rope bridge spanning a ravine, had to be made by foot. For the Beatles, who had scarcely had to walk to the front door since becoming stars in 1963, the contrast in lifestyle must have seemed dramatic.

It proved to be too dramatic for some.

Though the group were regarded as honoured guests, and given facilities altogether grander than those offered to their fellow students, the regime of exotic, if unvaried, food and perpetual assault from enormous flying insects took its toll.

This was the final occasion on which all the Beatles were gathered in one place with their original choice of lifelong partners — in other words, Cynthia Lennon, Jane Asher, Pattie Harrison and Maureen Starkey. Maureen was the first to crack, and her unhappiness was just the excuse that Ringo was looking for. The Starkeys flew home in relief after just ten days. McCartney and Asher made it through a month, before Jane claimed a prior theatrical engagement.

The Lennons and Harrisons were in for the long haul, but their friend Alexis Mardas, 'Magic Alex' of the newly-formed Apple Electronics company, had other ideas. He persuaded the remaining Beatles that the Maharishi was less concerned with spirituality than with investigating other potential avenues of intercourse with his female students. With the same certainty that they'd greeted the Maharishi as 'The One', Lennon and Harrison now denounced him. They marched into his hut and announced that they were leaving. He asked why, and Lennon responded with one of his classic put-downs: "You're the cosmic one, you should know". Harrison had already celebrated the nearest town to the camp, Deradoon, in song. Now it became their salvation, as the home of the solitary taxi which could return them to civilisation.

Back in Britain, the Beatles didn't stop to lick their wounded pride. They had another crusade to launch: the Apple empire which would offer artistic freedom and financial support to promising creative spirits all over the world.

"It's a controlled weirdness," Paul explained vaguely to an American interviewer, "a kind of Western communism. We want to help people, but without doing it like a charity. We're in the happy position of not needing any more money, so for the first time the bosses aren't in it for a profit. If you come to me and say, 'I've had such and such a dream', I'll say to you, 'Go away and do it'."

"The aim isn't just a stack of gold teeth in the bank," John added. We've done that bit. It's more of a trick to see if we can get artistic freedom within a business structure — to see if we can create things and sell them without charging five times our cost." It seemed to them like the perfect antidote to the corporate capitalism which had been controlling and limiting their career since they signed to Parlophone in 1962.

But outside of Apple, the rest of the Western world's youth culture had other ideas. While the Beatles had been in Rishikesh, political unrest had broken out across western Europe.

Thousands of students who, five years earlier, would have been happily singing along to 'She Loves You' and 'I Want To Hold Your Hand', had now taken to the streets to demonstrate against American involvement in the Vietnam War, and what they saw as the repressive nature of capitalist society.

The demonstrations began in West Berlin in February, spread to London in March, and reached their pinnacle early in May in Paris. Meanwhile, America had also been rocked by a wave of student and socialist protests, which had won the support of the entire rock counter-culture.

Back from the spiritual disillusionment of their abortive meditation episode, the Beatles watched the mounting protests with some degree of bewilderment. "I don't care if the government is all fascist, or communist. I don't care. They're all the same", Lennon had told Hunter Davies before the Beatles left for India. When they returned, he and McCartney had flown to New York to publicise the setting-up of Apple to the mainstream American media. For all their talk of "Western communism", there seemed to be a mighty gulf between the Beatles and the generation of rock bands who had formed in their wake.

One of the ironies of 1968 is that the two songs which have come to sum up the revolutionary zeal of that spring of political discontent — the Beatles' "Revolution" and the Rolling Stones' "Street Fighting Man" — were both statements distancing their creators from the student protests. By October 1968, the radical magazine *Red Dwarf* was accusing the Beatles of being concerned only "to safeguard their capitalist investments". In the rock culture of the age, you could hardly imagine a worse insult.

Given Lennon's revolutionary political activities between 1970 and 1972, it wouldn't have been surprising if he'd been inspired to rush to the barricades and rally to the students' cause with a quick chorus of "We Shall Overcome". Even Mick Jagger managed an afternoon stroll around Grosvenor Square during London's fiercest 1968 demonstration, observing rather than actually protesting.

But for the moment, all the Beatles had other priorities. Lennon was becoming obsessed with Yoko Ono, who was rapidly teaching John to "free his mind instead" without the need for a giggling guru. Back from India, having been let down by the man he'd elected to be his father figure for the year, Lennon slumped into even deeper depression and seclusion inside his stockbroker belt home.

Meanwhile, Japanese avant-garde artist Yoko Ono was avidly pursuing him, ostensibly for exactly the kind of financial backing that Apple was being set up to provide. Intrigued by her unconventional work and challenging personality, Lennon invited her to visit him at home while Cynthia was out of the country on holiday. By the early hours of the morning, John and Yoko had recorded their *Two Virgins* album, described by John Robertson as "an audio verité record of a night's work, a jumbled assemblage of voices, distorted musical instruments, sound effects tapes and the hum of the home studio . . . Lennon merely set up several of his tapes and loops on various recorders, and then he and Yoko improvised over the top."

The transition from acidic rock'n'roll to the formless chaos of *Two Virgins* didn't come easily. "Lennon sounds ill at ease," Robertson noted, "tantalised by what he is doing but unable to turn off his irony." There was still a connection, though: "Amidst the crashing barrage of noise and the half-hearted attempt at catharsis, you can hear two cultures, two views of the world, in collision — the tight, ironic rock'n'roller and the sure-footed performance artist." When the tape recorder was turned off, the couple made love until dawn. Cynthia returned from her vacation to find herself exiled from Lennon's life.

Not surprisingly, given the natural conservatism of the British media, John's divorce and very public courting of Yoko Ono provoked an avalanche of criticism, much of it snide, sexist and racist. Shortly before he died, Lennon described the episode in some of his sharpest and most direct prose, in an essay called 'The Ballad of John and Yoko'. At the time, he'd tried his best to shrug off the hatred he (and particularly Yoko) had encountered from the British media. A decade later, the memory burned fiercer than ever, and John let rip at the "derogatory garbage" which was written by "a bunch of beer-bellied, red-necked aging hacks".

While Lennon was discovering that love and art could be satisfied by the same person, McCartney was pursuing his own lack of satisfaction in a similar fashion. When an American named Francie Schwarz arrived at Apple's first office in the spring of 1968, she was determined to capture Paul McCartney's imagination, if only with her idea for a film-script: "I thought, well, you've come this far," she wrote in a quickie memoir called *Body Count*, "he has to be there. So I went, and he was there." McCartney asked her out for lunch: "It dawned on me that he was more interested in flirting with me than in the movie. I had to make up my mind." And they began an affair, while McCartney was still officially engaged to Jane Asher.

In the midst of post-Rishikesh depression, romantic upheaval, and political turmoil, the Beatles began recording their longest, strangest and most diverse album.

In India, they'd devoted most of their spare time to songwriting, influenced to varying degrees by their meditation experiences, as John Robertson noted: "Harrison was already using his music as a vehicle for his spiritual beliefs; his experiences in India merely strengthened his commitment. McCartney seems to have remained untouched by the experience; or at least he wasn't able, or ready, to translate his thoughts into song. He approached the leisure time as a professional tunesmith, cranking out a series of well-crafted, rounded songs which revealed little of his inner life."

"Lennon did not find subterfuge as easy, however, or as satisfying; and the songs he wrote in India were necessarily a reflection of his own life. Seeing himself and the world with heightened clarity — induced as much by the absence of chemicals as by the Maharishi's teaching — he took the process of self-discovery he had begun with his prose writings and his songs on 'Rubber Soul' a stage further."

To prepare for the sessions, the four Beatles congregated at George Harrison's Esher home, armed with acoustic guitars, hand drums, and what sounds like a bumper crop of top-grade marijuana. Over the course of a long weekend, they cut four-track demos of around 20 new songs, almost all of which had been written in India. In mood, they varied from the playfulness of 'Piggies' to the angst of 'I'm So Tired', the ethereal grace of 'Dear Prudence' to the satirical thrust of 'The Continuing Story Of Bungalow Bill'. But every one of them emerged from this joyous weekend as a declaration of good vibes towards all mankind. Even Lennon's 'Revolution' ended up sounding like a Beach Boys party tune when the pipe of peace was passed around.

Several of the songs taped during these sessions didn't make it as far as the studio; one regrettable casualty was Harrison's 'Circles', a charmingly spiritual and melodic tune which he reserved for a solo album nearly a decade-and-a-half later. But having familiarised themselves with the rest, the Beatles arrived at Abbey Road studios on the afternoon of Thursday 30th May 1968, with no plan beyond recording until they felt they had finished.

There was one immediate change when the 'White Album' sessions began: there weren't four musicians in the studio, but five. The extra party was Japanese musician, artist and (by late May) inseparable confidante of John Lennon, Yoko Ono. 'Birds' had never been welcome visitors in the studio till then; wives or girlfriends, they had been expected to wait at home for their men to arrive back from the studio, usually at breakfast time, with a three-course meal ready as the front door was opened.

But Ono had been a functioning and (within New York's tempestuous, if small, avant-garde community) flourishing artist for longer than any of the Beatles, and she wasn't going to bow to their male chauvinism. Neither were the other three prepared to veto Lennon's decision; his original leadership of the band, and brusque turn of phrase if crossed, ensured that he was still treated with wary respect. So Yoko stayed, yawning her way through endless re-takes and overdubs, sticking close to John's side, and intervening only to criticise the Beatles for their lack of effort or experimentalism. Slowly, the atmosphere soured, to the extent that by the end of the year, John was moved to write and record — and issue, on a Beatles Christmas record — a macabre fairy-tale in reverse, that left no doubt about where his allegiances lay. Ironically, the fact that his complaint formed part of a seasonal gift to the group's fans meant that few people took it seriously, though John continued to refer back to this stab at "some of their beast friends" in interviews for the rest of his life.

Most galling for the other Beatles was the realisation that John was more ready to listen to Yoko's opinions than theirs.

With what they viewed as an 'intruder' at every session, the group's normal blunt honesty with each other effectively vanished. If Paul, George or Ringo attempted to argue with John, they either found themselves discussing the problem with Yoko instead, or discovered that John simply wasn't listening. George had recently told Hunter Davies that "The reason why we're all here is to achieve perfection, to become Christ-like. Each soul is potentially divine. This actual world is an illusion. It doesn't matter what happens, the plan can't be affected, even having wars or dropping an H-Bomb. None of it matters." If the H-Bomb didn't count, then there wasn't much reason to get worked up if John Lennon had skipped a session or two.

But the other two Beatles found the situation more strained. Francie Schwarz reported that "Paul's enthusiasm was shrinking. The recording sessions were strained. He came home drunk on the nights they had recorded a John or George song."

Ringo's reaction was quieter, but more direct. On 22nd August, early in a session that (as usual) stretched ten hours from early evening almost until dawn, he walked out of the studio with a few brief words. The Abbey Road engineers saw him leave, and watched the rest of the group shrug their shoulders and get on with the job of recording the rhythm track for 'Back In The USSR'. Paul McCartney slipped comfortably onto the drumstool, and work on the 'White Album' continued. Twelve days later, though, Ringo was persuaded to return, after the remaining Beatles sent him a note confirming that they thought he was the greatest drummer in the world. On his first day back in the studio, Lennon garlanded his drumkit in flowers.

Everyone who visited Abbey Road during those desperately long sessions in summer 1968 remembers the tension, the grim silence, the fact that the individual Beatles were huddled in separate corners of the studio complex, rather than collaborating as a band as they had in the past.

But - and it's the most significant 'but' in the Beatles career - the music they created that summer, together and alone, was as eclectic, inspired and daring as anything in their entire catalogue. No other artist or band in rock history has made a record like *The Beatles*, as it was simply titled on its late 1968 release. On one level, it's ironic that an album regarded by most observers as consisting mainly of solo material by all four of the group should have the Beatles' name as its title; on the other, it's only too appropriate, because *The Beatles* proved that these four musicians could command, master and surpass any pop or rock genre yet invented.

One of the harshest critics of *The Beatles* has always been its producer, George Martin (though he actually missed many of the sessions, leaving Chris Thomas in charge in his place). A vocal fan of the studio perfection of *Sgt. Pepper's Lonely Hearts Club Band* and *Abbey Road*, Martin disliked the fact that the double 'White Album' contained so much, and that the songs weren't crafted and polished into gem-like form. He's long expressed the view that the set should have been trimmed down to one album of certifiable classics, and that the dross — 'Revolution 9', no doubt, and probably 'throwaways' like 'Wild Honey Pie' and 'Birthday' as well — should have been consigned to the vaults.

It's easy to see why George Martin should feel that way: all his musicianly instincts must have reacted against the deliberately slipshod and almost audio-verité recording sessions for *The Beatles*, where most of the tracks feature studio chatter while the songs are in progress, and so many of the numbers are quirky vignettes that don't break down into the faithful verse/chorus/middle eight structure Martin loved.

But George Martin's edited version of *The Beatles* wouldn't have been the same record. Nor would it have compared with *Sgt. Pepper* or *Abbey Road*. The major strength of the album is its sheer diversity — the fact that it has breathtakingly beautiful ballads like 'Mother Nature's Son' and 'Blackbird' alongside eccentric singalongs like 'Wild Honey Pie' and 'Bungalow Bill'. And the 'amateurishness' of the recording, with its rough edges and false starts, its spoken asides and weird sound effects, was in many ways a reaction by *all* of the Beatles to the note-perfect nature of *Sgt. Pepper*.

If you break down the Beatles' albums between Lennon and McCartney compositions, on the understanding that the pair only wrote together very occasionally after 1963, you discover that John dominated the early records.
On *A Hard Day's Night*, for instance, he wrote almost every song. Likewise, he commandeered all the group's A-sides between 'A Hard Day's Night' and 'Day Tripper'.

By 1966, and *Revolver*, McCartney had closed the gap, with Harrison coming up fast on the outside; and from *Sgt. Pepper* onwards, it was the bassist who set the pace, often phoning John at the start of album projects to announce that he had enough songs for them to begin recording. Only then would John pull himself laboriously from his self-enforced stupor at home with Cynthia, and painfully start work.

Perhaps it was his break from Cynthia, and the creative spark provided by his new relationship with Yoko, but Lennon devoted more effort and inspiration to the 'White Album' sessions than to any Beatles project after 1965. And for the third album running, he effectively set the tone for the summer-long recording sessions with his very first offering.

The publication of Mark Lewisohn's *The Complete Beatles Recording Sessions* raised eyebrows when it revealed that work on *Revolver* in 1966 began with the album's most experimental track, 'Tomorrow Never Knows'. With its tape-loops and surreal soundscape, Lennon's song declared to the world that the acid-inspired Beatles had moved way beyond their more innocent 1965 selves.

That winter, when work began on what developed into *Sgt. Pepper's Lonely Hearts Club Band*, Lennon once again drew the outer boundaries of the project, with the intensely personal imagery and sonic playfulness of 'Strawberry Fields Forever'. *Pepper* may have been McCartney's record, and 'Strawberry Fields' was, of course, not included on the finished album; but Lennon's creative daredevilry threw open the horizons for his colleagues — and for himself.

So how did the sessions for *'The Beatles'* begin? With Lennon's 'Revolution', the slow, doo-wopping, semi-satirical arrangement of his suitably semi-radical statement of political uncertainty. In its edited, relatively naked state, 'Revolution 1', as it was titled on the album, scarcely seems like the most adventurous outing on the record.

But 'Revolution 1' was only half of what was recorded on that first afternoon in May 1968. In its unedited state, the Beatles' initial pass at 'Revolution' ran for a full ten minutes, descending from the superbly sloppy rendition of the song into a sound collage that approximated the sound of a society in dissolution. Taking these additional six minutes of anarchy as their canvas, Lennon, Ono and (briefly) George Harrison painted layer upon layer of noise, random conversation and feedback, as they attempted to capture the ferment of the spring's student protests on tape.

Few observers at the time could make any sense of 'Revolution 9'; even one or more of the Beatles was apparently dubious about the final value of the piece. But regardless of its success or otherwise, Lennon's most outlandish Beatles creation was an important statement in itself. It announced that everyone's expectations of what a Beatles record was supposed to be were too narrow. In future, Lennon was saying, the group could work with sound as well as songs. Like 'Tomorrow Never Knows' and 'Strawberry Fields Forever', 'Revolution 9' demonstrated that the Beatles didn't recognise the concept of artistic limitation. They could be anything they wanted — and more.

And so it proved over the next five months. Freed from the need to follow *Sgt. Pepper* with an equally tight and coherent concept album, the group let their imaginations range as widely and wildly as they could. No subject was too serious to be satirised; no joke too silly to be told. The result was 90 minutes of music that was sometimes hysterically funny, sometimes chillingly sad; often self-indulgent, but even more often inspired; and so wide-ranging that it seemed as if the Beatles were trying to capture the whole of Western popular music in one album.

Sgt. Pepper had been the perfect example of the Beatles working in unison to create great art. With *The Beatles*, they opted for entirely the opposite method: they worked alone, but secure in the knowledge that their joint identity was big enough to encompass everything.

This was the album on which Ringo Starr surfaced as a solo composer for the first time. He'd been attempting to mimic his more creative partners since 1963, which was when he revealed that he was working on a song called 'Don't Pass Me By'. But every time he arrived at a Beatles session with an idea for a number, the others howled him down, saying that he'd simply nicked the tune from an old Jerry Lee Lewis B-side. The sale at Christie's of a Ringo composing tape proved that his initial idea for any song always began with familiar country chord changes. If it wasn't Jerry Lee, then it was Johnny Cash . . .

So it's not surprising that Beatles press officer Tony Barrow reported early in the 'White Album' sessions: "Ringo's number was a country and western piece when it was started. It began with the working title of 'This Is Some Friendly', but that could easily be changed before the finished record is ready for release. Gradually, as it went through the rehearsal stage, the song and its arrangement took on more and more of a rock'n'roll influence, and the tempo became faster and faster." Eventually it mutated into — what else? — 'Don't Pass Me By'.

"I'm not the creative one, I know that," Ringo said early in 1968. "But people expect I must want to be. They write and say why don't I try. It can get you down, not being creative. You know people are thinking you're not the creative one. But out of four people, you wouldn't expect them *all* to be creative, would you? 50% is enough."

George Harrison's response to the idea that only two of the four Beatles were creative would probably not have been printable. For several years, he'd felt restricted by Lennon and McCartney's fertile creativity, and reckoned that no one paid enough attention to the potential of his own work. "The problem was that John and Paul had written songs for so long," he explained in 1977. "First of all, they had such a lot of tunes, and they automatically thought that theirs should be the priority. So I'd always have to wait through ten of their songs before they'd even listen to one of mine. That's why my first solo album, *All Things Must Pass*, had so many songs, because it was like I'd been constipated. I had a little encouragement from time to time, but it was a *very* little."

"I didn't have much confidence in writing songs because of that, because they never said, 'Yeah, that's a good song'. When we got into things like 'While My Guitar Gently Weeps', we recorded it one night and there was such a lack of enthusiasm. So I went home really disappointed, because I knew the song was good."

It was more than good, as Harrison knew; in fact, it proved to be one of the album's real keepers. But there was an element of doubt in his own mind about the relevance of his work as a rock musician. "The only thing which is important in life is Karma, that means roughly 'actions'," he explained that spring. "Life will all work out, as long as you don't bullshit. That's what I'm trying to do. I've got so much going forward now. I see so many possibilities. I'm beginning to know that all I know is that I know nothing."

A decade later, he admitted that his immersion in the Indian lifestyle, spiritual and physical, had led him to rethink his attitude to everything, including his role as a guitar player: "I'd been playing sitar for three years by then. And I'd only been listening to classical Indian music, and practising sitar — except for when we played in the studio, and then I'd just get the guitar out and just play, you know, learn a part and play for the record. But I'd really lost a lot of interest in the guitar." Which is one of the reasons why George's close friend, Eric Clapton, ended up playing the long solo on 'While My Guitar Gently Weeps'.

John Lennon was scarcely in the same position as George Harrison when it came to impressing his will on the Beatles. But by the summer of 1968, he too was beginning to feel restricted by the need to make three-minute pop records. "John has these crazy ideas all the time," Yoko told the press that summer. "He just didn't use them. It was just a personal joke for himself. He has about 20 ideas in 20 minutes. So I would say, 'Well, that idea is good, why don't you just do it?', and he had never thought of actually doing it, physically. The point is, when you do something, something happens. The concept is simple, but then you get all sorts of reactions and you've started something."

The shift in John's philosophy since the start of the year had been profound. Speaking to Hunter Davies shortly before the group went to India, Lennon saw his priorities in strictly spiritual terms: "We never thought about any big things. Now I can. I'm not interested in little stages now. Acting doesn't interest me any more. It's a waste of time for me. Writing, I've done that. I wanted to do a book, and I produced one, so that was it. I suppose now what I'm interested in is a Nirvana, the Buddhist heaven. I don't know much about it, or really understand it enough to explain it. George knows more.

"Studying religion has made me try to improve relationships, not to be unpleasant. It's not a conscious move to change my personality. Perhaps it is, I don't know. I'm just trying to be how I want to be, and how I'd like others to be."

Yoko's influence persuaded John that Nirvana was all in the mind, and that he ought to express himself in public rather than keeping his thoughts and creativity to himself. That philosophy guided his work on *The Beatles*, which was more eclectic than anything else he ever produced. Who else could have dared to tackle the *musique concrete* of 'Revolution 9' alongside the gentle 'Julia'? Who could have nailed the Maharishi with the sly wit that John brought to 'Sexy Sadie', or turned the spiritual difficulties of Mia Farrow's sister into the global love song that was 'Dear Prudence'. And who else could have returned from two months searching for Nirvana via meditation with a stack of desperate, self-doubting lyrics like 'I'm So Tired' and 'Yer Blues'?

Paul McCartney didn't touch either the spiritual highs or the depressed lows of Lennon's work during his Indian songwriting interludes. As ever, he married craft with inspiration to produce a collection of tunes that reached out to the public, rather than into his own psyche. With the ease of the practised tunesmith, he was able to draw on fragments of real life — the presence of Beach Boys singer Mike Love in the Maharishi's camp, for instance, or the time he spent with his shaggy sheepdog Martha — as the basis of songs like 'Back In The USSR' and 'Martha My Dear'. But they weren't actually *about* anything in his life, which is what helped make them so universally popular.

If Lennon had gone through the romantic turmoil that was McCartney's life in 1968, then the entire sequence of events would have been openly chronicled in song. From his engagement to one of Britain's favourite young actresses, Jane Asher, Paul had flirted with a New York photographer called Linda Eastman, moved in with visiting American Francie Schwarz, had to face the rage of Jane's mother, who came to collect her spurned daughter's belongings, and then cast Schwarz aside so that he could concentrate on Linda and her young daughter, Heather. His head must have been reeling under the layers of love and deception, but his musicianship neatly turned out uncomplicated love songs like 'I Will' and expressions of naked lust like 'Helter Skelter'. It's somehow ironic that on an album which featured two statements about political revolution by the Beatles, the deranged cult leader Charles Manson should have fastened on the scarcely-veiled sexual imagery of Paul's 'Helter Skelter' as his call to start wreaking havoc on Hollywood's well-heeled movie stars and socialites.

"We're all really the same person," was how Paul described the Beatles just before the 'White Album' sessions began. "We're just four parts of the one. We're individuals, but we make up together The Mates, which is one person. If one of us, one side of the mates, leans over one way, we all go with him or we pull him back. We all add something different to the whole."

The well-maintained unity of the Beatles was gradually starting to disintegrate, however, and no one felt the loss more keenly than McCartney.

From the beginning, he'd been the public relations man in the group, the one who'd persuade Lennon to go through another mindless meet-and-greet with the mayor of some godforsaken American city, or who would tease Harrison out of his sitar den and back into the hubbub of the Beatles' sessions.

On the 'White Album', though, he finally had the chance to indulge another side of Paul McCartney: the multi-instrumentalist who wanted the chance to pursue his own vision. Lennon may have joked about *Paul McCartney Goes Too Far*, but alone of the Fab Four, Paul was the Beatle who could realistically write, record and produce his own records single-handedly. Ringo's brief departure from the group gave him the opportunity to play drums behind John and George, but there were several other tracks on which Paul handled all, or almost all, of the instruments.

In fact, insiders were saddened by the realisation that in different parts of Abbey Road studios, the four Beatles could be working on three separate songs at the same time. But the results more than justified the change in working methods. It might even be true to say that if the same policy had survived into 1969, then the *Let It Be* debacle would never have happened, and the Beatles might have managed to keep their four increasingly diverse talents together under one heading for a year or two longer.

As it was, their summer's work from 1968 sold faster than any album in history up to that point. *The Beatles* swept out of stores around the world in numbers that even *Sgt. Pepper* couldn't match. And most reviewers, despite their misgivings about 'Revolution 9' and some of the slighter song fragments, were awestruck by the continuing development of the Beatles' talent. In a rare piece of self-congratulation, the group even included Tony Palmer's *Sunday Times* review on the back of the *Yellow Submarine* soundtrack album in January 1969.

In *The Times*, William Mann — the classical critic who'd first alerted the 'proper' musical world to the Beatles' potential with his talk of "Aeolian cadences" and "pentatonic clusters", once again reached for his superlatives. He admitted that, "Some of the tracks are scrappy or pot-boilers", but concluded that "the Lennon-McCartney songs are as provocative as ever. Nine of the 26 are superbly inventive, and in the same class is George Harrison's 'Long, Long, Long' — though, as with several other tracks, I am in two minds how much of the appeal is due to the brilliant scoring of George Martin (whom some regard as, not the fifth, but the first Beatle).

"There are too many private jokes (they remind me of the Beyond-the-Fringe revues) and too much pastiche to convince me that Lennon and McCartney are still pressing forward with their race against other progressive composers. The genius is all there, though . . . It is, once again, a brilliant feat of invention. The next Lennon-McCartney anthology must, imperatively, look forward rather than back. But these 30 tracks contain plenty to be studied, enjoyed gradually appreciated more fully, in the coming months. No other living composer has achieved so much this year."

Poet Adrian Mitchell was even moved to verse by the vision of the Beatles circa 1968:

"I'm not trying to paint you a quartet of saints
or musical Guevaras.
But the standard of loving has
plopped through the bottom of the graph.
So the few who do any kind of thing
that shakes out the horrors
are quadruply welcome
especially if they make us laugh."

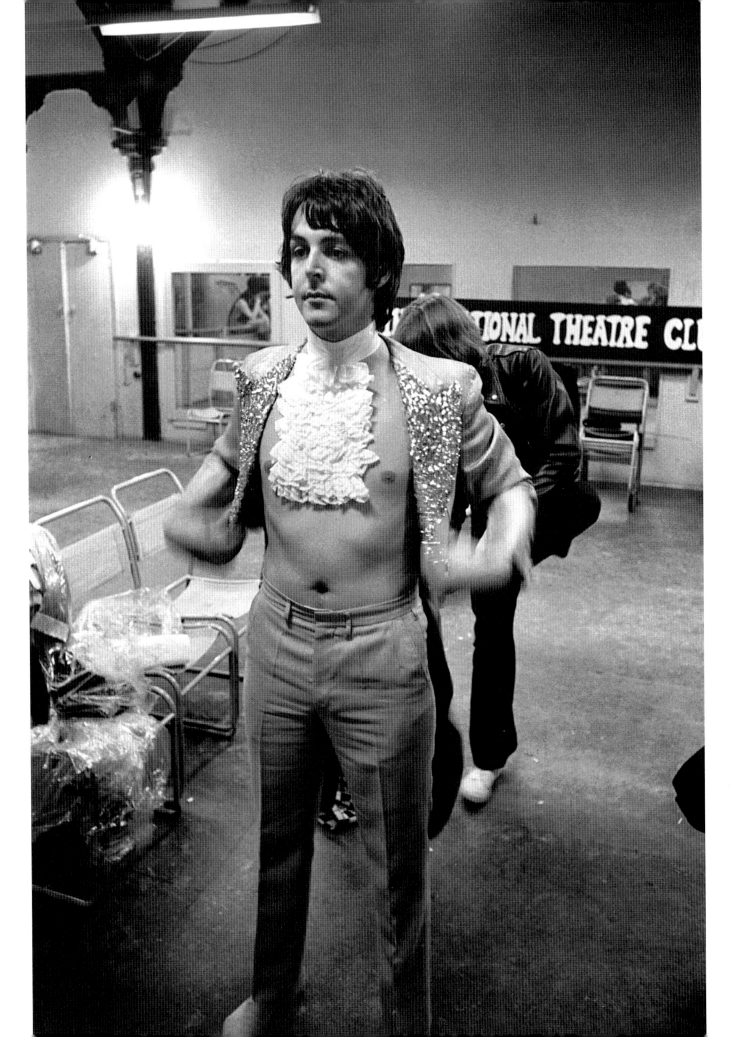

Brilliant though *The Beatles* was, if there was one record in 1968 which helped the world to "shake out the horrors", it was the first release on the Apple label: 'Hey Jude'. Coupled as it was with a fuzz-guitar arrangement of Lennon's 'Revolution' which rivalled 'Helter Skelter' as the Beatles' rawest rocker ever, 'Hey Jude' can still lay claim to be not only the group's best double-sided single, but maybe the best of all time. You could certainly be forgiven for thinking that 'Strawberry Fields Forever'/'Penny Lane' is its only real contender.

Francie Schwarz remembers that 'Hey Jude' was the tune which obsessed Paul McCartney in the late spring and early summer of 1968, noting in her book that whenever he had a spare moment, he ended up at the piano tinkering with the chords and lyrics. Right up to the moment he recorded his final vocal in the studio, McCartney wanted to rewrite the words: only Lennon's insistence that lines like "the movement you need is on your shoulder" had a resonance that surpassed the fact that they really didn't mean anything stopped him short.

Lennon had his own reasons for looking favourably on the song. Though Paul has claimed a thousand times that it was inspired by John's son Julian, a five-year-old having to struggle through the bitter and all too public divorce of his parents, John swore blind to the end of his life that it was really about him, and that his longtime musical collaborator was wishing him all the best for his new life with Yoko.

The beauty of the song — like the best of McCartney's work down the decades — is that the exact inspiration doesn't really matter. With the melodic genius that came heaven-sent throughout the Beatles' career, Paul succeeded in composing a melody that was both joyously happy and desperately sad. When the Beatles recorded it with an endless fade-out that turned 'Hey Jude' into the anthem of the late 60s — maybe the last moment on which they really captured the attention of the entire world — the song seemed so vast and all-encompassing that all anyone could do was buy it. And buy it millions did, making it the group's best-selling single of all time, rightfully so.

To mark such an auspicious happening, the Beatles agreed to perform both sides of their new single live in a TV studio before a small audience, creating what were in effect promotional videos a decade before their time. Hedging their bets a little, they followed the lead of their 'live' recording of 'All You Need Is Love' the previous summer, and used instrumental backing tracks, which also featured a single lead vocal for each song. In front of the cameras, the group mimed their guitarwork and drumming, while John howled out a second lead vocal for 'Revolution', and George and Paul offered some metallic doo-wops in support.

That was a straight performance clip, thrilling to watch, but without any audience interaction. 'Hey Jude' was something else. Paul sat behind a live piano, and duplicated his lead from the record, while the others mimed with their hands and sang with their voices once again. Midway through the song, the stewards let the audience through, and for the first time in their lives, the Beatles were suddenly performing not just to their fans, but in the middle of them. If you look back at the clip again, you'll notice that half the audience seem to have been struck almost dumb with amazement; the other half are almost deliriously happy.

As the mass chorale sang more and more rounds of the final chorus, Lennon turned his microphone round towards the fans. The following year, he launched his new solo project with the slogan: "You are all the Plastic Ono Band". On that afternoon in Teddington TV studios, and then a few days later when the 'Hey Jude' clip was seen around the world, we were all The Beatles. It was the finest, most poignant moment of a year of mind-boggling extremes — and unforgettable music.

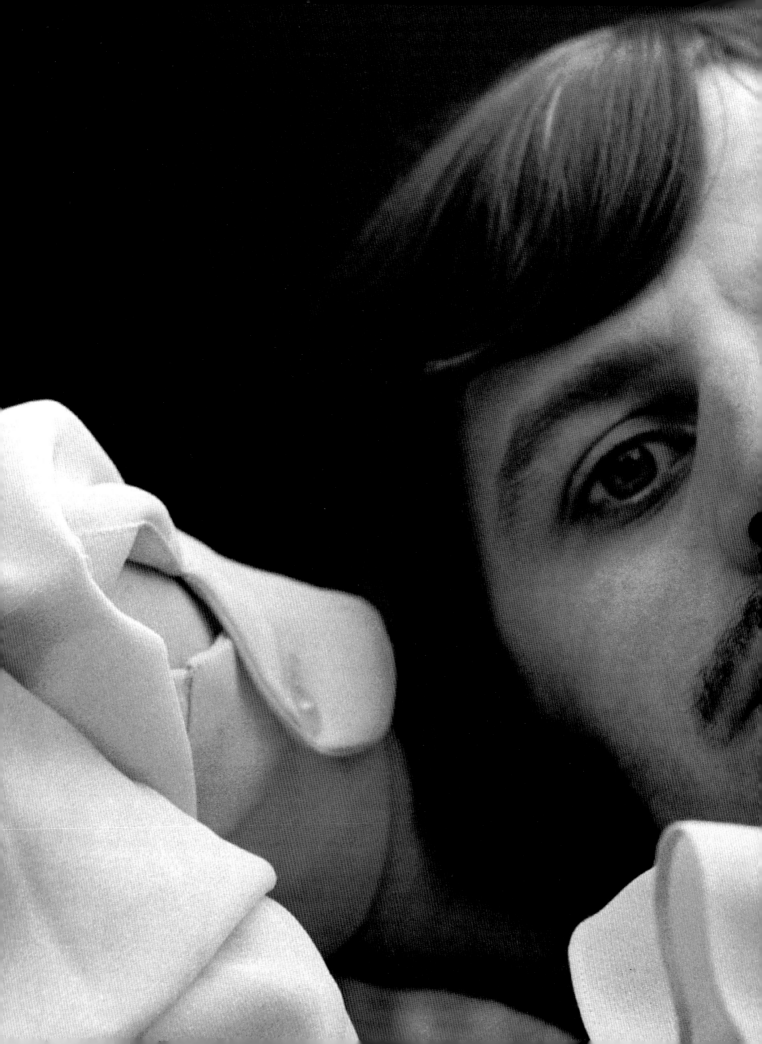

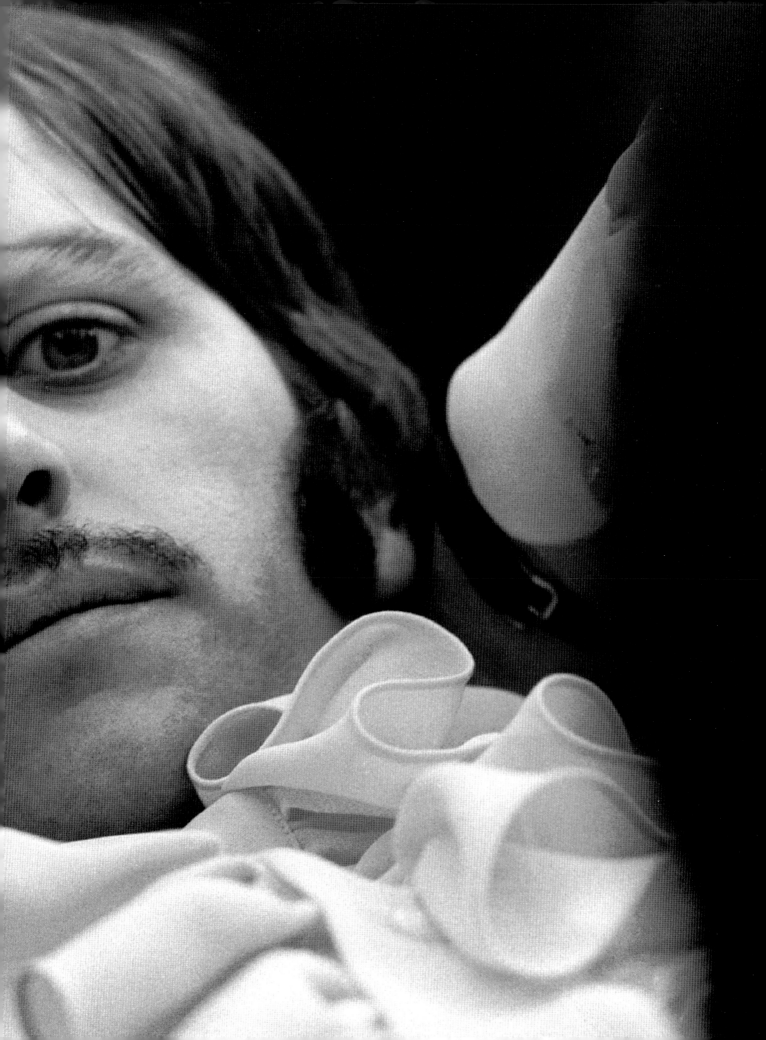

'The Beatles Mad Day Out'

On Sunday July 28th, taking advantage of their customary weekend breaks during the 'White Album' sessions, the Beatles congregated in central London for a photo session. Five years earlier, they had regularly been glimpsed around the West End, striking the daft poses that were required for the anodyne pop press of the time. They'd allowed themselves to be photographed with a bizarre variety of props, from deerstalker hats to table-tennis bats, and even agreed to romp up and down the sea-front at the Somerset resort of Weston-super-Mare in striped Edwardian bathing costumes.

By 1968, it was an achievement to gather all four Beatles in the same location, let alone with a photographer in tow, and no-one suggested any bathing costume shots. It turned out to be one of the Beatles' final joint photo sessions — and by all accounts it stunned the Sunday afternoon tourists and strollers who witnessed four of the world's most famous faces striding towards them unannounced.

There to capture his slice of history was Don McCullin, a young photographer who was about the same age as George Harrison. Only a few years into a rising career as a freelance photographer, he was allowed the kind of intimate access to the group that the rest of the world's lensmen would have beaten each other to death to obtain. Accompanying Don was his friend and fellow photographer, Tom Murray.

"The idea", wrote Beatles roadie Mal Evans a few weeks after the session, "was to get together a whole new collection of pictures, really good ones, from which the fan clubs could have fresh supplies. This time The Beatles were determined to do something a bit better than just putting their four heads together in front of a wall."

....spread like tiny insects over the giant glass lens of McCartney's geodome.

The quartet gathered around midday —
an early start for the Fab Four — at McCartney's home in St. John's Wood.

"John came with me in my car," Mal Evans recalled, adding that he'd brought his young son Gary along for the outing. "The others piled into Ringo's white Mercedes, and a van carrying all the different costumes and clothes trailed behind us as we crossed London from St. John's Wood through the West End to Fleet Street and beyond. The first stop was the 'Sunday Times' building, where we used the roof to do the first set of pictures. And we used a wind machine to get nice effects on the fellows' hair. In fact, I think it helped to produce some of the first group photographs to show all four Beatle foreheads uncovered beneath windswept hair!"

Five years after the initial media frenzy about the group's terrifyingly hirsute appearance, the exact shape of their haircuts still guaranteed plenty of press attention. It's difficult from this perspective to imagine the publicity which was given to these famous shots of four Beatles standing with their foreheads exposed to the elements. Their fashionably untutored hair was swept casually back from their faces, while the quartet posed in theatrical capes — McCartney carefully adorning his with a Liverpool FC rosette. Other shots in the same location saw the Beatles adopting mock-cartoon poses, as if they'd suddenly been thrown back into a more innocent age, and asked to recreate the playing-field scene of *A Hard Day's Night*.

The afternoon's second location was the Mercury Theatre near Notting Hill Gate. There they posed with a parrot and a piano for a series of shots that were used throughout 1968 whenever there was a new record to promote. Watched by the disbelieving theatre staff, McCartney donned a circus-like costume which was reminiscent of the *Sgt. Pepper* cover, and banged away at the upright, while Harrison and Lennon — George clad in harlequin's trousers like a psychedelic humbug — casually sat on the top of the piano. A second series of shots was taken in the theatre's bar.

"From there," Mal Evans explained, "we went East again, stopping in a suburban residential area to do a few street shots in front of houses, before heading for the London docks. Paul stripped to the waist, exposing just the barest hint of Beatles flab, and at one point posed provocatively with some dockyard chains.

There were some park shots to follow, "in one of the borough parks in Highgate," Murray recalls. "The hollyhocks were over seven feet tall, and I took a picture of the boys among them. It was later turned into quite a famous poster. I also took some shots of the Beatles sitting with a tramp on a park bench. I don't think the tramp had any idea who they were!"

Then, as Mal Evans recalled, "we returned to St. John's Wood and Paul's house for more tea and the last lot of photographs. This time Paul's massive dog Martha got into the act, like she always does. Paul had the ideal spot for picture-taking. We trooped down to the foot of his garden. There, hidden away behind all the trees, Paul had this fantastic glass dome." And there the Beatles were arranged for the final photographs of the afternoon, spread like tiny insects over the giant glass lens of McCartney's geodome.

THE BEATLES

the summer of 1968

PHOTOGRAPHIC CREDITS

© Don McCullin/Magnum pages: 3, 4, 5, 7, 8, 9, 10, 11, 12, 13, 14, 15, 16, 17, 18, 19, 21, 22, 35, 37, 38, 39, 41, 42, 43, 44, 45, 46, 49, 50, 51, 52, 53, 54, 55, 56, 57, 58, 60, 61, 62, 63.

© Tom Murray. Book cover and pages 25, 26, 27, 28, 29, 30, 31, 33.

T R A © K S

For more information contact:
Tracks, P. O. Box 117 · Chorley · Lancashire · PR7 2QZ · England
Tel 01257 269726 · Fax 01257 231340
E-Mail · TRACKS@PROVIDER.CO.UK